JUST WILD ENOUGH

Mireya Mayor, Primatologist

Marta Magellan

illustrated by
Clémentine Rocheron

ALBERT WHITMAN & COMPANY
Chicago, Illinois

As always, in honor of my grandson
Sammy Joseph Schnall—MM

Dedicated to all the people who want to
create a life full of passion, love, and freedom,
spreading light on their own path—CR

Library of Congress Cataloging-in-Publication data
is on file with the publisher.
Text copyright © 2022 by Marta Magellan
Illustrations copyright © 2022 by Albert Whitman & Company
Illustrations by Clémentine Rocheron
First published in the United States of America
in 2022 by Albert Whitman & Company
ISBN 978-0-8075-4085-5 (hardcover)
ISBN 978-0-8075-4086-2 (ebook)

Printed in China
10 9 8 7 6 5 4 3 2 1 WKT 26 25 24 23 22

Design by Aphelandra

For more information about Albert Whitman & Company,
visit our website at www.albertwhitman.com.

From Mireya Mayor

I grew up in Miami, a big city with few opportunities for exploration and nature. But my love and curiosity for animals began as soon as I could crawl. I love travel and adventure, but what I love even more is protecting animals that are on the verge of extinction. I make TV programs about wild places and animals in hopes of inspiring the next generation of explorers. And while I didn't "look like a scientist," I never let anyone discourage me from pursuing my dream. It's important that we follow our dreams and try to make a difference, even when those dreams seem too wild to become a reality. I am a living example that all dreams are possible, and that no dream is too wild.

Mireya Mayor's house teemed with critters,
raggedy cats that strayed into her yard,
waggly-tailed dogs that followed her home,
rabbits, birds, snapping turtles,
and a chicken named Maggie.

Mireya adopted the worms, snails, and beetles
burrowing and scurrying outside.
And sheltered them under her bed.
But the brown anole lizards darted by too fast.
She needed a closer look.

A dandelion stem
tied with a loop at
the end was just
the thing.

SWOOP!
Got it!

Mireya examined the lizard, just as
a scientist would, and set it free.
Her house was like a wild kingdom.
But not quite wild enough.

Camping in the woods would be wild.
Mireya asked Mami if she could join
the Girl Scouts.

"And sleep outdoors at night?" Mami said.
"Too dangerous!"
So Mireya took ballet lessons instead.

As she grew, Mireya's dancing
got better and better.
Twirling and whirling,
she spun like a tornado,

waved like an ocean,

and leaped like a gazelle.

While in college, Mireya auditioned to be a cheerleader
for the National Football League.
Waving pom-poms in front of 75,000 Miami Dolphins fans thrilled her.
The cheering crowd was wild.
But not quite wild enough.

Mireya wanted to hang with primates:
gorillas, monkeys, chimpanzees,
orangutans, baboons, lemurs.
Her dreams roared as loud as the crowds
at the football games.

"I'd like to be a primatologist," Mireya told her college professor.
The instructor told Mireya she would have to do work in a jungle.
Awesome!
In pink hiking boots, a black designer vest, and flaming red lipstick,
she felt quite wild enough.

Not everybody agreed.
Mami wanted Mireya to follow her dreams
but not camp in a dangerous jungle!
Mireya's cheerleader friends understood she needed a change.
But why trade in pom-poms for hiking boots?
Some researchers told her she didn't look like a scientist.

But what does a scientist look like, anyway?

So, dreaming louder than all the doubters, Mireya plunged into a South American jungle to study a rare monkey.

But wading in swamps
brought trouble.

A blood infection!

Mireya's hands swelled into red and purple balloons.

The doctors said she almost died.

Back home in the hospital, she daydreamed of her next wild adventure.

But dreaming wasn't quite wild enough.

On the far-flung island of Madagascar,
far, far away from anywhere Mireya had ever been,
there lived a rare primate, almost extinct.

Nobody had ever studied those
inky-black lemurs up close.
Nobody had ever photographed them.
Nobody thought Mireya would go.

But she did.

So many hissing, giant cockroaches,
screaming geckos,
and creatures that looked like Dr. Seuss characters.
The place looked wild enough.
Mireya felt right at home.

While in Madagascar, *National Geographic* hired her as its very first woman wildlife TV reporter. With the cameras rolling, she explored.

Giraffes in Namibia!

Great white sharks in the Pacific Ocean!

Gorillas in the Congo!

The media called her the female Indiana Jones,
a whip-cracking professor from the movies.
It was as wild as it could get.
But it wasn't quite wild enough.
Not for Mireya.

So, with another researcher, she hiked deep
into the mountains in Madagascar,
inside one of its last virgin rain forests,
to record every wild creature they could find.
But one tiny lemur had them stumped.
Mireya needed a closer look.

Night after night Mireya placed bananas inside a trap. Morning after morning, the trap was full of fruit flies, but nothing quite wild enough.

One rainy evening, a surprise. The tiniest of all primates, a mouse lemur, shivered inside. Got it!

Mireya nestled the sopping-wet lemur in her shirt pocket.

Leaping over tree roots, she dashed back to camp.

She drew some of its blood and analyzed the samples.

What a discovery!

Neither a western nor an eastern mouse lemur—it was a new species!

But Mireya saw trouble ahead.

The little primate lived in a threatened habitat.
Fires burned up and down the hillsides.
People were stripping the trees from the rain forest for fuel.
The lemur's home wouldn't stay wild enough for long.

To protect the endangered lemur,
Mireya met with Jacques Sylla, the prime minister of Madagascar.
With her usual passion, she rooted for the mouse lemur's survival.
And she posed a wild idea.
Could the area be declared a national park?

The prime minister
wondered and pondered,
and finally—

"We can do it," he said.

The government declared the lemur's rain forest a protected area.

The tiniest of primates with one cheerleader-turned-scientist
helped save a threatened wilderness.
Which would now and for a long time to come
remain quite wild enough.

Glossary

brown anole: A small lizard native to Cuba and the Bahamas. It is highly invasive and has largely displaced the native Carolina, or green, anole.

endangered: At serious risk of becoming extinct.

extinct: When there are no more individuals of a species alive anywhere in the world.

habitat: A place where an animal lives. There are many different sorts of habitats all over the world, from forests to deserts to mountains. Different habitats are home to different animals.

lemur: A type of primate found only on the island of Madagascar off the east coast of Africa. Lemurs live in trees and have enormous eyes and long, furry tails.

mouse lemur: The smallest living primate in the world. It can fit inside a teacup (or an explorer's pocket).

primates: Members of a group of mammals that includes humans, apes, monkeys, and lemurs. The largest primate is the gorilla. The smallest is the mouse lemur, which weighs as little as 1 ounce, about the same as a pencil. All primates have certain physical features in common, such as large brains, eyes that face forward, nails instead of claws, and hands that are able to grasp things because their thumbs can touch their fingers.

primatologist: A scientist who specializes in studying primates.

species: A group of similar living things that are able to reproduce with other members of the group.

Author's Note

I first heard of Mireya Mayor when her former poetry professor, Ricardo Pau-Llosa, suggested we interview her for *Miambiance*, a literary magazine at Miami Dade College. Years later, my critique group partner, Aixa Perez-Prado, told me Mireya was now the director of exploration and science communication at Florida International University and suggested I contact her.

What a life Mireya has had! She was born in Miami, Florida, in 1973. Her mother raised her with help from her grandfather, grandmother, and aunt. Mireya's dream of becoming a primatologist came true after receiving her first grant to study the endangered white-faced sakis in 1996. She reached another milestone when she received her PhD from Stony Brook University, specializing in endangered primates and conservation. With geneticist and veterinarian Edward Louis, director of the Omaha Zoo's Madagascar Biodiversity Project, she co-led an expedition to Anjanaharibe-Sud in northeastern Madagascar, now a protected area. The media still calls her the female Indiana Jones, and, like the movie hero, she is a university professor. Married with six children, Mireya lives in Miami but travels around the world speaking about her wild adventures and the importance of conservation.

About Mouse Lemurs

Mouse lemurs are a rarity in primate research. Primatologists, like Mireya, and residents of Madagascar have helped to make sure the mouse lemur habitats are protected. Mireya worked closely with the prime minister there, leading to a new national preserve to be set aside so that mouse lemurs and other species could survive. Afterward, the government tripled the size of the protected areas to save even more endangered species from people deforesting their habitats. Although lemurs aren't supposed to be hunted, some people still capture them to sell as exotic pets.

Several more species of lemur have been identified since Mireya's discovery, some in the last few years. Scientists have counted dozens of species of mouse lemurs. More research needs to be done to identify all the separate species. In addition to her work with the mouse lemur, Mireya was the first scientist to take samples from an inky-black lemur, the Perrier's sifaka, and the all-white silky sifaka, a critically endangered lemur with a very small number in the wild and none in captivity.

Anjanaharibe-Sud Special Reserve

Deep in the remote and rugged mountains of northeastern Madagascar, this reserve contains some of the last intact stands of virgin rain forest left in middle and high elevations in the country. In this reserve live an amazing variety of rare plants and animal species found nowhere else. The survival of many of the endangered species is directly linked to the preservation of forests such as Anjanaharibe-Sud, which is now managed by Madagascar National Parks.

Other Books

De la Bédoyère, Camilla. *100 Things You Should Know about Monkeys & Apes*. New York: Gareth Stevens, 2016.

Goodall, Jane. *The Chimpanzee Children of Gombe*. New York: Michael Neugebauer, 2014.

Gregory, Josh. *Lemurs*. New York: Children's Press, 2017.

McManus, Lori. *Gorillas*. Chicago: Heinemann Library, 2012.

Acknowledgments

I'm grateful first of all to Professor Ricardo Pau-Llosa for introducing—and Professor Aixa Perez Prado for reintroducing—me to Mireya Mayor. As always, my SCBWI Miami critique group helped with the initial versions, and my online nonfiction 12X12 group helped with later versions. Many thanks to my agent, Kortney Price, for her enthusiasm and conviction that this story was indeed quite wild enough and should be published. Finally, I am thankful to Mireya Mayor, who was so gracious in our phone calls and texts, and whose autobiography provided me with much vicarious pleasure, because what nature-loving girl doesn't dream of being an explorer?